THE WORLD OF

FLIGHT

Ian Graham

KINGFISHER

BOSTON

D1468266

KINGFISHER

a Houghton Mifflin Company imprint
222 Berkeley Street
Boston, Massachusetts 02116
www.houghtonmifflinbooks.com

First published in 2006
10 9 8 7 6 5 4 3 2 1

1TR/0206/TIMS/PICA(PICA)/128MA/F

LIBRARY OF CONGRESS CATALOGING-IN-PUBLICATION DATA
has been applied for.

ISBN 0-7534-6008-4
ISBN 978-07534-6008-5

Senior editor: Clive Wilson
Art director: Mike Davis
Cover designer: Jack Clucas
Production controller: Teresa Wood
DTP manager: Nicky Studdart
Picture manager: Jane Lambert
Indexer: Hilary Bird

Printed in China

The Publisher would like to thank the **Royal Aeronautical Society** for
their help and co-operation in the production of this book.

Since its formation in 1866, the Royal Aeronautical Society, the oldest
aeronautical learned society in the world, has played a key role in the
development of aviation, aeronautics and aerospace technology. Its
worldwide membership is drawn from all aerospace professions, and
ranges from students to captains of industry. Further information
about the Society can be obtained from its web site:
www.aerosociety.com

All views expressed are the author's own.

CONTENTS

CIVIL AVIATION

In a little less than 100 years, airplanes have evolved from flimsy wood and wire contraptions into technological marvels, flying millions of passengers around the world. The first regular airline services began soon after the end of World War I (1914–1918) when bombers were converted into passenger aircraft. By the 1930s all-metal monoplanes such as the Boeing 247, the Lockheed Electra, and the Douglas DC-3 were much faster and more comfortable for those who could afford air travel. The first jet airliner, the British de Havilland DH106 Comet, which had 44 seats, entered service in 1952. The first American jet airliner, the 147-seat Boeing 707, flew five years later and helped make air travel affordable and popular. At the end of the 1960s a new type of airliner—the wide-bodied jet—was introduced. Today there is a huge range of commercial aircraft, from small business jets and helicopters to the massive Airbus A380.

Dawn of a new age
The first modern airliner
was the Boeing 247, which
was introduced in 1933.
It was a metal monoplane
with retractable wheels
and an enclosed cabin with
seats for ten passengers.

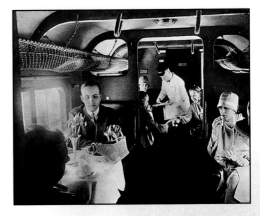

Airliners

Every day thousands of airliners crisscross the skies.
They include tiny island hoppers and commuter
planes, with room for only a few passengers, as well
as some of the world's largest aircraft, which can carry
hundreds of people. One of these, the Boeing 747 jumbo
jet, has flown more than two billion passengers over 28
billion miles (45 billion km) since it was first introduced
in 1969—and the more recent Airbus A380 can seat
up to 480. These airliners are so huge that the entire
distance of the first flight made by the Wright
brothers could be flown inside the length of one 747!

Sky trains
During the 1920s air travelers sat
in passenger cabins that were designed
like first-class railroad cars—which is how
wealthy passengers usually traveled. Airplanes
flew in the rough air below 16,400 feet
(5,000m), much lower than they do today,
so flights could be very uncomfortable.

Jumbo size
One of the biggest airliners in service is the
Boeing 747-400. It has a maximum capacity of
up to 568 people, although it typically carries
420 passengers. This enormous aircraft is 230
feet (70m) long, has a wingspan of 210 feet
(64m), and can weigh up to 395 tons at takeoff.

A breath of fresh air

Airliners cruise at a height of about 42,500 feet (13,000m). At this altitude the air can be as cold as -76°F (-60°C) and too thin to breathe. However, airline passengers do not have to wear oxygen masks like fighter pilots, because airliner cabins are pressurized. Air is compressed by the engines and then temperature-controlled. It is then pumped into the passenger cabin. The first pressurized airliner, the Boeing Stratoliner, began flying in 1940.

Twentieth-century classic

Although it was designed as an airliner, the Lockheed Constellation first saw service as a military transporter during World War II. After the war it was reconverted to an airliner. The "Connie" had beautiful, curving lines and a distinctive triple-fin tail. Early models carried only 60 passengers. Bigger versions were built well into the 1950s.

Faster than sound

In 1976 a revolutionary new airliner took to the skies. The Concorde was the first civil airplane that could fly faster than sound. It represented a huge leap forward in airliner technology. Cruising at 1,335 mph (2,150km/h), more than twice the speed of sound, it slashed long-distance flight times in half. A subsonic airliner flies from New York to London in around seven hours. The Concorde could fly the same route in only 3.5 hours. Even the most advanced fighter planes could not match the Concorde's performance.

Glamorous Glennis
Charles "Chuck" Yeager (b. 1923) stands beside the Bell X-1 rocket plane. On October 14, 1947, Yeager made the first supersonic flight in the X-1. He reached a speed of 698 mph (1,126km/h). The record-breaking plane was named *Glamorous Glennis* after Yeager's wife.

Sonic booms
As the Concorde accelerated through the speed of sound, air piled up in front of it, forming a shock wave. A second shock wave formed at the tail. The shock waves reached the ground, making a double bang, or sonic boom, as they passed over.

Future Concordes
The Concorde went out of service, but aircraft manufacturers are designing new supersonic airliners. Computer simulations are used to study the way air flows around them (right). The Concorde's successor will be bigger, quieter, and powered by engines that are less harmful to the environment.

Nose of distinction
The Concorde's distinctive nose was pointed so that it could punch through the air at twice the speed of sound.

As the Concorde began its descent prior to landing, its visor slid down into the nose to reveal the cockpit's windshield.

Finally, the nose itself was lowered to give the crew a better view of the ground. This nose-down position was also used for takeoff.

Supersonic power plants
At full power the Concorde's engines generated 70 tons of thrust, more than twice the maximum thrust of the biggest jumbo jet. During a flight across the Atlantic Ocean, its four Rolls-Royce/SNECMA Olympus jet engines burned around 80 tons of fuel.

Tough tires
The Concorde's speed at takeoff was 248 mph (400km/h). This is faster than any other airliner—a Boeing 747, for example, takes off at 198 mph (320km/h). The Concorde's tires had to be incredibly strong. To make the rubber extra tough, it was reinforced with steel cables. If a tire burst, the pieces could damage the aircraft. In July 2000 a tire bursting on takeoff probably caused an Air France Concorde to crash, killing everyone on board. All Concordes were grounded while designers and engineers investigated ways to prevent a similar tragedy from happening again.

Building an airliner

Airliners are among the most complex machines ever built, and they are assembled inside some of the largest buildings on earth. The main Boeing jumbo jet production hall in Everett, Washington, is 1,968 feet (600m) wide and nearly 1,640 feet (500m) long—the equivalent of 56 football fields! Each plane is made from as many as six million parts. More than 10,000 people work around the clock to produce about five jumbo jets in a month. When each one has been built, the finishing touches are added, which are the seating and paint scheme ordered by the airline. Finally the airplane is ready to be flight-tested and then delivered to the airline.

The assembly hall

Airbus airliners (main picture) are made in sections by 30,000 workers all over Europe. The cockpit and center section of the aircraft are made in France, the rest of the fuselage in Germany, the tail in Spain, and the wings in the U.K. Engines come from the U.K. and the U.S. The sections are joined together and the aircraft are completed in a cavernous hangar in Toulouse, France.

Close inspection
Airlines and their pilots are closely involved in the development of a new airliner. They are invited to inspect mock-ups and prototypes of the new aircraft.

New for old

Airliners undergo regular maintenance and servicing. Every part of the airplane has a built-in life expectancy so that it can be replaced before it breaks down. Depending on the type of aircraft, an airliner is completely rebuilt every four to eight years. It is taken apart and stripped down to the bare metal. Any faulty parts are repaired or replaced. Then the airplane is put back together again and repainted. The whole process can take up to three months.

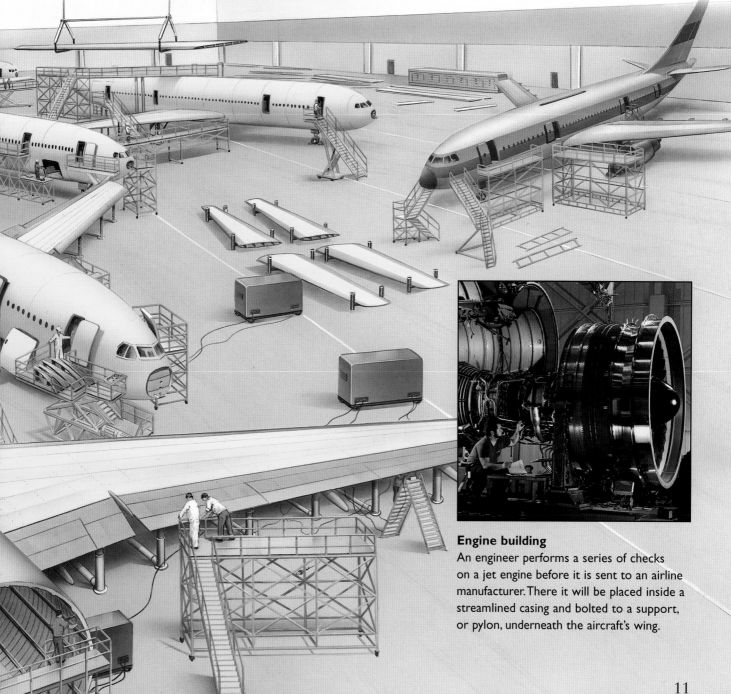

Engine building
An engineer performs a series of checks on a jet engine before it is sent to an airline manufacturer. There it will be placed inside a streamlined casing and bolted to a support, or pylon, underneath the aircraft's wing.

Igor Sikorsky (1889–1972)
The first successful helicopter was the VS-300. It was built in the United States in 1939 by the brilliant aircraft engineer and Soviet immigrant Igor Sikorsky.

Spinning blades

The idea of building a vehicle that flies vertically (straight up) dates back to the 1300s. But it took another 600 years before the technology became available to make this a reality with the invention of the helicopter. Instead of wings, helicopters have long, thin blades, called rotors. When they spin, the blades cut through the air and create lift, even when the helicopter is not moving forward. This allows helicopters to fly in ways that are impossible for fixed-wing aircraft. Their ability to take off vertically, fly in any direction, and hover (stay in one spot in the air) make them ideal for all kinds of tasks. Helicopters are used for rescue work, military transport, and even flying business executives to and from heliports atop city office buildings.

The tilt-rotor
The tilt-rotor can fly like a fixed-wing craft but can take off and land like a helicopter. It has wings and very large propellers called prop-rotors.

As a tilt-rotor prepares to land, its engines slowly tilt up. The prop-rotors start to provide some of the lift instead of the wings.

The aircraft slows down, and, with the engines pointing straight up, it can hover and land in a confined space, just like a helicopter.

Leonardo da Vinci
The Italian artist and scientist Leonardo da Vinci (1452–1519) made one of the earliest drawings of a helicopter in about 1500. His sketch shows a design for a corkscrew-like propeller. He thought the device would spin up into the air when the screwlike propeller turned.

Speed restrictions

Helicopters pay a price for their amazing flying abilities—they cannot fly as fast as fixed-wing aircraft. Whirling rotor blades create much more air resistance than a smooth, thin wing. Also, a high proportion of the engine power has to produce lift instead of propelling the aircraft through the air. As a result most helicopters fly at just 124–186 mph (200–300km/h), compared to 310–434 mph (500–700km/h) for a small, twin-turboprop aircraft. However, a type of aircraft called a tilt-rotor overcomes this by using long propellers that also work as rotors.

A tilt-rotor takes off vertically, and it can hover like a helicopter. Its engines then swing forward, and the rotors become propellers. A tilt-rotor can fly at speeds of 310 mph (500km/h).

Flood rescue

A Kawasaki BK 117 helicopter winches people to safety from a treetop during the disastrous floods that swamped large parts of Mozambique, in Africa, during February 2000. The water rose so fast that there was little time to escape, and thousands of people were trapped on roofs and in treetops. Helicopters were the only aircraft that could reach them quickly.

A plane for all seasons
The Dornier 228 light transport plane is a popular choice for air services in remote places. It can take off from fields, and when fitted with skids, it can land on snow. It is used as a passenger plane, a cargo freighter, an air ambulance, and a maritime patrol aircraft.

Flying doctors
The huge distances between homes in the Australian outback mean that often the only way to get medical help to people quickly is by air. In 1928 Rev. J. Flynn founded the Royal Flying Doctor Service, which uses light planes to fly doctors to wherever they are needed.

To the ends of the earth

In many of the remotest parts of the world, the only practical way to get around is by air. Communities on the polar ice caps and in the Australian outback, for example, depend on aircraft for essential supplies and emergency services. Even more isolated are offshore oil rigs or gas platforms. These rely mainly on helicopters to ferry workers to and from the mainland and to carry supplies. Each rig has a helipad, a platform where helicopters land. Amphibious aircraft, which can land on water, are particularly useful in places like Canada, where there are a lot of lakes and rivers on which to land. Seaplanes also provide air links between far-flung islands.

Flexible fliers

Aircraft that fly to remote places are chosen because of their special capabilities or because they are modified to cope with extreme conditions. Short Takeoff and Landing (STOL) planes are often used because they can take off from and land on very short runways or landing fields. They are sometimes fitted with extra fuel tanks because they may not be able to refuel where they land. Aircraft flying to the polar outskirts are fitted with skids, or skis, to spread their weight over a larger area and to stop them from sinking into the snow.

Going home

A Sikorsky S-61N Sea King transport helicopter takes off from an oil rig's helipad, carrying oil workers home to the mainland for a well-earned break. The Sea King's watertight, boat-shaped body allows it to land on water in an emergency.

Fighting fires

The Canadair CL-415 is a twin-engined amphibious plane. Its boat-shaped hull and floats under the wings enable it to land on water. It also has wheels for landing on a runway. The CL-415 was designed as a fire-fighting aircraft to protect Canada's forests. While skimming a lake, it can take 1,586 gallons (6,000l) of water on board in only 12 seconds.

FLYING FOR FUN

In the early days of aviation, flying circuses thrilled the crowds. Air races also proved to be an exciting sport for pilots and spectators and helped speed up the development of aircraft technology. The flying circuses have gone, but air races are still held, and they are as competitive as ever. Aerobatics have grown in popularity because of the amazing maneuvers the pilots can perform. As commercial aviation developed in the 1950s and 1960s, so did competitive and recreational flying. Elegant gliders, small piston-engine aircraft, thoroughbred racers, and nimble aerobatic planes were built and flown in increasing numbers. The variety of aircraft available for competitive and recreational flying has never been greater. Ultralights and hang gliders enable almost anyone to enjoy the thrill of flight, while new technology is giving the earliest types of aircraft a new lease on life. The oldest of all, hot-air balloons, have become popular again; airships, the first aircraft to offer luxury air travel, are taking to the skies once more.

Aerial sports

Pilots can compete against each other in two ways—racing and aerobatics (air acrobatics). Air races helped encourage the development of new, faster planes in the early years of aviation. Pilots could win valuable cash prizes and trophies. In 1920 the winner of the Schneider Trophy flew at 107 mph (172km/h); the 1931 winner reached a top speed of 339 mph (547km/h). Today the National Air Races are held near Reno, Nevada. Aerobatic contests are not about speed. Instead, the focus is on flying skills and performing difficult maneuvers. Pilots fly individually or in teams, making their planes tumble and roll in carefully planned maneuvers.

Roll over
The Pitts Special is a very popular choice for aerobatics and stunt flying. Its short fuselage and biplane wings make it a very strong and agile performer. With a flick of the joystick, the pilot can roll the aircraft all the way around in just over one second!

The Schneider Trophy
Supermarine seaplanes (above) won the Schneider Trophy (right) three times between 1927 and 1931. The contests were invented by Frenchman Jacques Schneider in 1913 to speed up the development of new seaplanes.

The pursuit of power

All kinds of aircraft compete in air races, from historical biplanes to finely tuned racing craft. World War II fighters, such as the North American P-51 Mustang, the Lockheed P-38 Lightning, and the Hawker Sea Fury are still flying today as racing planes. The small size, low weight, and high-powered engines that once made them fearsome fighters also make them ideal racing machines. To make them even faster, every bit of unnecessary weight is removed. The engine is tuned and tweaked to achieve maximum power. Even the exterior receives special attention— it is polished to a mirror finish to help the plane slip through the air as fast as possible.

Racing at Reno
A P-51 Mustang leads the pack as it banks around a tower, or pylon, during the annual air races in Reno, Nevada. Several courses for different racing classes are marked out by the pylons. The slowest biplanes race on the three-mile (5-km)-long course. The longest course, more than eight miles (13km), is reserved for the Unlimited racing class, which the fastest planes enter.

Light aircraft and gliders

Light aircraft are the taxis of the aviation world. With room for three or four passengers and a top speed of no more than 186 mph (300km/h), they are ideal for short flights up to 620 miles (1,000km). As well as recreational flying by private pilots, they carry tourists on sight-seeing tours and are often used as air ambulances. The lightest aircraft of all are ultralights, hang gliders, and gliders. Gliders and hang gliders are generally unpowered. They soar on rising currents of air, which their pilots become experts at detecting. Fun to fly, light aircraft give thousands of people their first taste of piloting an aircraft.

Foot-powered takeoff
A hang glider pilot takes to the air. This type of hang glider has a stiff wing. Others are made from a metal frame covered with flexible material that billows into a wing shape when filled with air. Pilots turn hang gliders to the left or right by shifting their weight to one side. Speed can be controlled by tipping the wing up or down.

Air tourism
A Piper PA-23 Aztec gives its passengers a bird's eye view of the Grand Canyon. The twin-engine Aztec has been providing air taxi, recreational, tourism, and business services for 30 years, and it is still widely used today for training new pilots.

Ultralight plane
An ultralight plane prepares for landing. The pilot sits in an open cockpit and flies the plane with the same stick and pedal controls that are used by other light aircraft.

Light and maneuverable
Ultralights are small, low-cost, and lightweight powered craft. There are two main categories of ultralights—weightshift and three-axis control. Weightshift craft are steered by the pilot shifting their weight in the same way as a hang glider pilot. Three-axis craft have flying controls like larger aircraft. They may have an enclosed cockpit, and there are even seaplane and flying boat versions for landing on water. The lightest type of ultralight is a powered parachute. This is a long, slender, wing-shaped parachute powered by an engine and a propeller, which are strapped to the pilot hanging underneath it.

Thermals
Gliders can climb by circling inside rising columns of warm air called thermals. Air rises when it is warmed by land that has been heated by the sun and when wind is deflected up by hills.

Soaring in silence
Gliders are made of strong but lightweight materials such as glass-reinforced plastic. Once a glider has been launched—either by catapult from the ground or by towing it aloft—it can stay airborne for many hours.

Lighter than air

Airships and balloons are able to fly because they are lighter than the air around them, even though they are made from materials that are heavier than air. They manage this seemingly impossible task by carrying a huge bag full of lighter-than-air gas. The lifting force, or buoyancy, of the gas overcomes the craft's weight, and it floats up. Most airships use helium, a nonflammable gas, while most balloons use hot air, which is lighter than cold air.

Historic day
The first crewed flight in an untethered craft was made on November 21, 1783. Jean-Francois Pilâtre de Rozier (1756–1785) and Francois d'Arlandes (1742–1809) drifted across Paris in a hot-air balloon built by Étienne and Joseph Montgolfier.

Hot and cold
A hot-air balloon gains height when the air inside it is heated by a gas burner. This creates lift. To descend, hot air is released through a vent and replaced by cooler, heavier air.

Fire hazards
Airships are lighter-than-air, powered vessels that can be steered. During the 1920s and 1930s they flew passengers in great comfort and style across oceans and continents. However, there was always the risk of fire because most airships were filled with hydrogen, which catches fire easily. A series of disasters during the 1930s, as well as the beginning of World War II in 1939, ended the age of passenger airship travel. Today airships are making a comeback using helium, a less flammable gas than hydrogen.

End of an era
As the giant German airship *Hindenburg* came in to land at Lakehurst, New Jersey, on May 6, 1937, it caught on fire. Of the 97 crew and passengers on board, 5 died.

Birth of the airship

The first crewed airship was built and flown in September 1852 by Henri Giffard (1825–1882), a French engineer. A propeller driven by a steam engine was attached to the hydrogen-filled balloon.

Return of the airship

A modern airship glides over a city. It is powered by two propellers, which can be tilted to make the airship climb or dive. The body, or envelope, of the airship is filled with helium gas. Air bags, called ballonets, inside the envelope allow the helium to expand safely as the craft climbs.

AIR SAFETY

Safety is the top priority at every stage of aircraft design, manufacture, and operation. International safety regulations ensure that air travel is one of the safest forms of transportation. The most important onboard systems are duplicated, so if one fails in flight, there is at least one backup—and usually more than one—to take over. Onboard computers detect faults quickly and alert the crew. If an aircraft develops a serious problem, safety equipment—ranging from oxygen masks and life jackets to escape chutes and fire fighting systems—help protect the crew and passengers. Combat aircraft also have ejector seats to let the crew escape quickly.

On the ground, air traffic controllers play a crucial part in air safety by making sure aircraft remain a safe distance apart. On the very rare occasions when a plane crashes, the causes are investigated and analyzed in great detail to help prevent similar crashes from happening again.

Controlling the skies

An airliner's crew steers a course by using radio signals from beacons on the ground and satellites orbiting the earth. Air traffic controllers track aircraft movements and give the crew permission to change height and direction when necessary. The controllers are able to see exactly where the aircraft are by using radar. This uses radio waves reflected by an aircraft to show its position on a radar screen. Each plane transmits information about itself, and this also appears on the screen.

GPS satellite
Aircraft can locate their position using GPS satellites. Each satellite orbits the earth about every 12 hours at a height of 12,000 miles (18,000km). Its solar panels generate 800 watts of electricity to power its communications equipment.

Ground control
An airliner's movements are directed by air traffic controllers from the moment it leaves the terminal building. Aircraft on the ground are guided from the airport's visual control room, a room with large windows in the control tower overlooking the runways.

Satellite navigation

Airliners pinpoint their position by measuring the direction to radio beacons (transmitters) in known positions on the ground. However, there are large parts of the world where there are no radio beacons, so most airliners now also use a satellite navigation system that covers the whole world. The Global Positioning System (GPS) consists of 24 satellites orbiting earth. Using radio signals transmitted by any four satellites, an airliner can find its position accurately.

Flying by eye
In the early years of aviation, aircraft rarely flew out of sight of land, so pilots could steer a course by using a map and compass. They also followed well-known landmarks on the ground, such as rivers, towns, railroads, valleys, and coastlines.

Skyways
Airliners can fly automatically from one place to another, using navigation satellites and beacons to update their flight computers. Airplanes fly through invisible airways, or "air corridors," 11 miles (18km) wide and 980 feet (300m) apart vertically.

Air hazards

All forms of transportation involve some level of risk. Aircraft, just like other complicated machines, can occasionally break down. In addition to mechanical or electrical problems, such as fires and engine failure, aircraft are affected by extreme weather such as storms and lightning. They also run the risk of collisions and terrorist attacks. However, the hazards involved in air travel are well known and dealt with so effectively that accidents are very rare. Statistically, you would have to fly one trillion miles before becoming a victim of a fatal accident.

Comet catastrophe
When three de Havilland Comets, the world's first jet airliner (top), crashed in 1953 and 1954, all Comets were grounded. Air crash investigators pumped a Comet full of water again and again (above) to simulate the effect of air pressure during a flight. The fuselage cracked open, revealing that metal fatigue was the cause of the accidents.

Midair disaster
On April 28, 1988, part of an Aloha Airlines Boeing 737's fuselage tore off during a flight to Honolulu, Hawaii. In thin air at a height of 24,000 ft. (7,300m), air pressure inside Flight 243 ripped open its fuselage, weakened by a crack.

Wind shear

A sudden change in wind direction or speed, called wind shear, can rob a plane of lift and height. This is very dangerous when a plane is near the ground and can result in a crash. Wind shear is often caused by downward wind from a rainstorm called a microburst. Airliners now have wind shear warning systems on board.

Flight recorders

Large airliners carry two machines that record information about the plane and the way it flies. The flight data recorder records information, including the plane's height, speed, direction, pitch (how much its nose is tipped up or down), and how fast it is climbing or diving. The cockpit voice recorder records the last half hour of the pilots' voices and other sounds on the flight deck. In the event of a crash these recorders provide vital clues to why the accident happened. The recorders are built to survive a crash, fire, and immersion in water.

Black boxes are not black
An airliner's flight recorders are known as "black boxes," but they are actually orange. Their distinctive, bright color makes them much easier to find.

Safe landing
Passengers are evacuated from Aloha Airlines Flight 243 immediately after its emergency arrival at Kahului Airport on Maui. Even though the plane was so badly damaged, the pilot was able to make a normal landing. Of the 95 people aboard, one flight attendant died.

Blind flying

By the 1930s aircraft instruments gave pilots enough information to fly without the need to look outside. However, it was very dangerous for pilots to practice blind flying, as this is called, in real aircraft. Early flight simulators, such as this one, were used to teach blind flying in safety.

Flight simulators

Pilots are trained to cope with every imaginable situation. They rehearse in-flight emergencies again and again. And using flight simulators, they can do this without ever actually leaving the ground. A flight simulator is an exact copy of the inside of a real plane's cockpit. The pilots look out at a computer-generated view and experience every movement as if they are really flying. Flight simulators teach pilots how to deal with dangerous situations without risking real aircraft. They are also much less expensive than taking airliners out of service for training flights.

Virtual flying

Modern flight simulators stand on computer-controlled legs. They tilt the simulator in different directions to give pilots the sensation of flying. The pilots are cut off from the real world. They see, hear, and feel only the virtual world created by the computer.

Going nowhere

A training officer sits at a control desk behind the pilots inside a Boeing 747-400 flight simulator. It is identical to the 747-400's flight deck. The trainer can test the pilots' skills by recreating a huge range of different conditions, from bad weather to potentially catastrophic faults in the aircraft.

Digital airports

A flight simulator's computer system is programmed with digital copies of the world's major airports. So when a simulator crew approaches Hong Kong or New York, they see what appears to be the real landscape and airport. The training officer can make things more difficult for them by adding fog, crosswinds, wind shear, rain, or dozens of other weather effects and any of 500 different equipment failures. In fact, flight simulators are so good that pilots can qualify to fly aircraft in them before ever flying the real plane.

AIRPOWER

Airpower is a vital part of modern warfare. Controlling the skies over a war zone is frequently the key to winning the ground war. Aircraft went to war only eight years after the Wright brothers made the first powered flight. In 1911 Italian forces used a Blériot plane to spy on Turkish troops in North Africa. During World War I (1914–1918) new kinds of warplanes were designed and built, including fighters, bombers, transport planes, and ground attack aircraft. When helicopters were developed in the 1930s, they provided military forces with a new type of weapon. Today there are warplanes that can fly at more than twice the speed of sound, stealth planes that can fly to their targets without being detected, and transport planes big enough to carry more than 100 tons of cargo.

Air combat

A successful fighter plane has to be fast and agile to outmaneuver enemy aircraft in a dogfight. Since the first pilots fired at each other with revolvers and rifles during World War I (1914–1918), fighter firepower and speed have developed at a furious pace. World War I fighters could manage a top speed of 105 mph (170km/h). During World War II (1939–1945) many fighters were topping 434 mph (700km/h) and carried up to eight machine guns. The first jet fighters, introduced at the end of the war, could reach 558 mph (900km/h). Today the fastest fighters streak through the sky at 1,483 mph (2,400km/h) and have an awesome arsenal of weapons.

Dangerous adversary
The German Fokker D.VII (left) was one of the most effective fighters of World War I. It was rushed into service in the spring of 1918. The Fokker D.VII could survive a lot of damage, and it was also easily repaired. Its main strength was that it handled very well at high altitude—up to 20,000 feet (6,100m), where other aircraft found it difficult to fly.

Fighting for France
A French-built Spad S.13 (right) banks away from danger. A total of 8,472 Spad S.13s were built and flown by several air forces.

The Spitfire
The Supermarine Spitfire was the most important British fighter of World War II. More than 20,000 of them were built. It had a top speed of 445 mph (720km/h) and was armed with up to eight machine guns. With the Hawker Hurricane, the Spitfire helped Britain's pilots win the Battle of Britain in 1940.

From machine guns to missiles

A faster fighter can close in on its enemy and get out of trouble more quickly, but it cannot turn as tightly as a slower plane in a dogfight. As fighters have become faster, they have had to be able to attack each other from farther away. Machine guns were a fighter's main weapon until the 1950s, when air-to-air missiles (AAMs) were introduced. Some of these missiles can now home in on a target up to 186 miles (300km) away from the attacking plane.

Fighting Falcon
The F-16 Fighting Falcon (left) was developed in the United States in the 1970s as a small, agile fighter for close combat. The F-16 has a wingspan of 31 feet (10m), not much more than a World War I fighter, but it has a top speed of over 1,320 mph (2,146km/h).

The Eurofighter
The Eurofighter EFA 2000 has been developed by the U.K., Germany, Italy, and Spain. Computers play a big part in operating the plane. The pilot can select a target just by looking at it and can activate a weapon by talking to the plane's computer.

The "flying wing"
In 1946 the American aircraft manufacturer Northrop built a bomber, the XB-35, in the shape of a wing. It was followed by the jet-powered YB-49 in 1947. Forty years later the flying wing design was brought back for the B-2 Stealth Bomber.

The black art of stealth

Stealth planes seem to appear out of nowhere and can surprise an enemy, with devastating results. These strangely shaped aircraft have a cloak of invisibility that allows them to slip through enemy radars undetected. Stealth planes, such as the B-2 Spirit and the F-117 Nighthawk, use special paint and materials to reduce radar reflections. Their carefully designed shape makes any remaining reflections from enemy radar systems bounce away.

Northrop B-2
The Northrop B-2 Spirit is more commonly known as the Stealth Bomber. Guided by satellite, it is designed to get through enemy air defenses without being detected and to deliver up to 80 bombs or 16 missiles to key targets.

Flexible fighter
The Joint Strike Fighter is a multirole stealth warplane being developed for the U.S. Air Force, Navy, and Marine Corps and the U.K. Royal Navy. The JSF will have short takeoff and vertical landing ability and will be able to climb nearly one mile in under ten seconds. It is expected to enter service in 2008.

Iron-ball paint

One way of reducing radar reflections from an aircraft to make it more "stealthy" is to cover it with a special paint called iron-ball paint. This contains billions of microscopic iron balls that absorb radar signals. The balls allow the electric currents produced by the radar to flow through the paint, so less energy is reflected. Iron-ball paint is black when cold, but it turns blue when it heats up during flight.

DarkStar

DarkStar is an unpiloted reconnaissance aircraft (spy plane) flown by remote control. It can fly at a height of more than eight miles (13km), and its shape makes it even stealthier than the F-117 or B-2.

F-117 Nighthawk

The F-117 Nighthawk is covered in flat panels that bounce radar signals away from an enemy transmitter. The engines' exhausts are broad and flat to make the hot gases mix well with the cool air and reduce the chance of heat detection.

Laser accuracy

The F-117 is armed with laser-guided bombs or missiles stored in two bays inside its body. When a weapon is released, a laser beam is fired at the target. The weapon locks onto the beam and flies to the target with pinpoint accuracy.

Dressing for action

Airline pilots and passengers fly in everyday clothes, but military pilots and astronauts have to wear special uniforms just to survive. A military pilot wears a helmet to protect the head during extreme maneuvers. An oxygen mask clips to the helmet. A G suit, or partial pressure suit, fits over their flying suit. In tight turns the G suit inflates like a balloon, applying pressure around the lower half of the body. This stops blood from draining out of the head and pooling in the legs. Without the G suit the pilot would black out. Astronauts wear helmets and suits that completely cover their bodies, sealing them inside their own mini-atmosphere.

Wool and cork
In 1908 an American showman, Samuel Franklin Cody, made the first official airplane flight in Britain. His "uniform" was a cork helmet, a thick wool coat, and leather boots.

"Eye" tech helmet
This special helmet tracks eye movements, allowing a military helicopter pilot to aim weapons just by looking at the target. Information can also be projected onto the visor so that the pilot does not have to look down at the instrument panel.

Combat clothing
Every piece of a military aircrew's equipment is important. In addition to the helmet, oxygen mask, flight suit, and G suit, a life preserver is essential. If a landing in the ocean is unavoidable, it inflates with gas to keep the crew member afloat.

Lifesaver

Today every fighter pilot wears a parachute. Until the 1930s, however, many military fliers chose not to wear a parachute, even though this meant that there was no escape if their planes went down. Pilots believed that they had a better chance of survival by trying to land their planes rather than by trusting a flimsy piece of material. Attitudes changed just before World War II. During the war about 100,000 aircrew were saved by parachutes.

Highfliers

The crews of high-flying planes such as the Lockheed SR-71 Blackbird have to wear a helmet and a full pressure suit—similar to a space suit. The suit protects their bodies from the thin, freezing atmosphere.

X-15

PUSHING THE LIMITS

Today aircraft fly higher, faster, and farther than ever before. Advances in aircraft design depend on pioneering pilots, researchers, and designers who are constantly pushing the boundaries of aviation technology. The outer limits of an aircraft's performance are called its flight envelope. Test pilots fly every new aircraft to discover its flight envelope so that other pilots can fly it safely. When the Boeing 747 jumbo jet was designed, it underwent 1,500 hours of test flights, using five aircraft over ten months, before it entered service with the world's airlines. Advances in aviation technology are often made by building experimental aircraft. These aircraft are not intended to go into production, but are built to test new developments.

X-1

X-29

A series of experimental aircraft called X-craft have been
built in the United States since the 1940s. The X-1 was the
first aircraft to break the sound barrier, in 1947. The X-15 was
an experimental rocket plane. Existing aircraft are sometimes
used as flying test beds for new engines or wing designs,
or to test parts made from new materials.

The Wright brothers

On the morning of December 17, 1903, Orville Wright (1871–1948) lay down on the lower wing of the plane that he and his brother, Wilbur (1867–1912), had designed and built. The engine was started, and the twin propellers spun up to speed. The plane accelerated along a wooden rail and rose into the air. It flew for 12 seconds and landed 120 feet (36m) away. The two brothers had made history. It was the first controlled flight in a piloted machine taking off under its own power.

Otto Lilienthal (1849–1896)
The German aviation pioneer Otto Lilienthal made more than 2,000 glider flights before he was killed in 1896 when his fixed-wing glider stalled. His work to control a wing in flight inspired other pioneers, including Orville and Wilbur Wright.

Flyer No. 2
By 1904 the Wright brothers were making routine flights of over five minutes. They built three different models called *Flyer*, then a two-seat model called the *Type A*.

Flight controls

The pilot of a Wright brothers' plane steered in two ways. He made the plane climb or dive by pulling a lever to tilt a pair of elevators at the front. He turned the plane by sliding to one side or the other. The pilot lay in a slinglike cradle linked to the wingtips by wires. Sliding to one side moved the cradle and made one wingtip twist one way while the other twisted the opposite direction. This made the plane roll into a turn. Later Wright planes had a seat for the pilot, and the sliding cradle was replaced with a lever.

Making history

Orville Wright eases the first *Flyer* airplane into the air on December 17, 1903, at Kill Devil Hill near Kitty Hawk, North Carolina. Between them, Orville and Wilbur Wright made four flights that day, the longest lasting 59 seconds and covering over 850 feet (260m). It took another four years before European pioneers equaled this achievement.

Flying contraption

The Marquis d'Equevilly demonstrates his "multiplane" in 1908. He mistakenly believed that aircraft should have as many wings as possible. After the Wright brothers' success in 1903, many pioneers in Europe attempted to build working airplanes.

Trailblazers

Today airline passengers travel in comfort, protected by an array of navigation and safety systems. But in the early years of flight, pilots often risked their lives trying to be the first to fly the routes that modern airliners use. From Louis Blériot's historic crossing of the English Channel to Charles Lindbergh's epic journey across the Atlantic Ocean, pioneering flights were usually made in difficult and dangerous circumstances. This was the era of the great trailblazers—pilots whose groundbreaking flights played a key role in the development of aviation.

Flying the English Channel
On July 25, 1909, Louis Blériot made the first airplane flight across the English Channel. He took off from Les Baraques, France, in his Blériot XI aircraft and landed 36 minutes later at Northfall Meadow, England.

The pioneers
By the 1920s intrepid aviators had reached every continent. They proved that airplanes were a practical means of long-distance transportation. The new air services that followed carried mail at first, then passengers.

Louis Blériot 1909

Alcock & Brown 1919

Charles Lindbergh 1927

Amelia Earhart 1932

Amy Johnson 1930

England
English Channel
France

Europe

North America

Asia

Atlantic Ocean

Africa

South America

Indian Ocean

Australia

Louis Blériot
(1872–1936)

John Alcock
(1892–1919)

Arthur Brown
(1886–1948)

Charles Lindbergh
(1902–1974)

Amelia Earhart
(1898–1937)

Amy Johnson
(1903–1941)

The lure of the Atlantic Ocean

The greatest challenge for early aviators was flying across the northern Atlantic Ocean. This route linked the most important business centers at that time—New York, London, and Paris. In May 1919 a U.S. Navy flying boat crossed the ocean in stages for the first time. One month later two British Royal Air Force pilots, Captain John Alcock and Lieutenant Arthur Whitten Brown, made the first nonstop flight across the North Atlantic. In a Vickers Vimy bomber, they took just under sixteen and a half hours to fly from St. Johns, Newfoundland, to Clifden, Ireland.

A hero in the making

Charles Lindbergh's plane, *Spirit of St. Louis*, skims the waves during the first nonstop solo flight across the Atlantic Ocean in 1927. He took off from New York on May 20 and landed in Paris 33.5 hours later. The flight made him famous overnight.

Flying to fame

In 1932 Amelia Earhart was the first female aviator to fly solo across the Atlantic Ocean. Three years later she made the first solo flight from Hawaii to California. Tragically, she disappeared over the Pacific Ocean in 1937, while trying to fly around the world.

Spy in the sky

In 1976 the Lockheed SR-71 Blackbird reached a speed of 2,189 mph (3,350km/h). This remained a world record for a jet aircraft until 2004. The Blackbird was designed as a spy plane that could fly so fast and so high, no enemy aircraft or missile could catch it or shoot it down. It had a crew of two. A pilot in the front cockpit flew the aircraft, while a navigator, who also operated the spying equipment, sat behind him. Today the Blackbird is used for scientific research and testing high-speed propulsion systems.

In-flight refueling
A Blackbird takes on fuel from a tanker plane. During a flight a Blackbird has to be refueled every two hours. NASA has two Blackbirds, which carry out experiments at a height of more than 85,000 feet (26,000m).

Top secret
A Blackbird accelerates to its trisonic (three times the speed of sound) cruising speed. The Blackbird was first flown in 1964. Missions usually lasted two to five hours, and its spy cameras could survey 101,400 square miles (260,000km^2) of the earth's surface every hour.

Dancing diamonds
Fiery "dancing diamonds," caused by shock waves in the engines' exhaust jets, stretch out behind a Blackbird as engine power is boosted to maximum.

Spiky engines
The Blackbird's extremely powerful engines have a unique design. A spike at the front of each engine moves forward or backward to let in exactly the right amount of air.

Heat-resistant
The Blackbird flies so fast that air rushing past it heats parts of the aircraft to temperatures of up to 932°F (500°C). Its exterior is made almost entirely from titanium, a metal that can withstand very high temperatures without melting. Metals expand when they heat up. The thin surfaces of the Blackbird's wings are folded like an accordion. When the Blackbird is on the ground, you can see the fuel leaking from gaps in the wings, but in the air the wing surfaces heat up, expand, and flatten, sealing the gaps.

Parachute
A Blackbird touches down on the runway at 174 mph (280km/h) and releases its braking parachute. This giant parachute creates air resistance, which slows down the aircraft.

Seattle

New York

Andrews Air
Force Base

Chateau
d'Oex,
Switzerland

Dakla, Egypt

BREITLING
ORBITER 3

Circling
the globe

In the early history of aviation
the ultimate distance goal was the
race to be the first around the world.
This was first achieved in the 1920s,
but the planes had to keep landing to
refuel. Records were quickly broken—
the first solo flight around the world,
the fewest number of stops, faster
and faster times. But it was not until
1986 that the first nonstop around-
the-world flight without refueling
was made by *Voyager*. Many failed
attempts were also made to fly a
balloon around the world. In 1999
the Breitling *Orbiter 3* balloon finally
succeeded and set the last great
aviation record of the 20th century.

Cruising around the world
Two U.S. Army Air Service crews, flying Douglas
World Cruiser single-engined biplanes, made the
very first around-the-world flight in 1924. The
trip took 175 days and covered 27,500 miles
(44,340km), with 72 stops on the way.

	Douglas World Cruisers 1924
	Winnie Mae 1933
	Voyager 1986
	Breitling *Orbiter 3* 1999

Lucky Lady

The first nonstop around-the-world flight was achieved in 1949 by the U.S. Air Force. A Boeing B-50 Superfortress called *Lucky Lady II* made the 24,000-mile (37,740-km) flight in 93 hours. The aircraft had to be refueled in the air four times. In-flight refueling was specifically created for this record-breaking flight.

Breitling *Orbiter 3*
The Breitling *Orbiter 3* balloon, with Bertrand Piccard and Brian Jones on board, took advantage of a high-altitude wind, or jet stream, to float 30,000 miles (48,000km) around the world in 19 days.

Wiley Post (1900–93)
The first solo around-the-world flight was achieved by the American Wiley Post in 1933. He flew his Lockheed Vega, called *Winnie Mae*, 15,500 miles (25,099km) in less than eight days, starting and finishing in New York City.

Voyager
The first nonstop around-the-world flight without refueling was made by Dick Rutan and Jeana Yeager in 1986. The 25,000-mile (40,212-km) flight took place in their experimental airplane, *Voyager*, in just over nine days.

Third stage

Second stage

First stage

Beyond the atmosphere

A new chapter in the story of flight began when
the Soviet Union launched the first artificial satellite,
Sputnik 1 in 1957, and sent the first man into space
in 1961. They were launched on top of rockets, the
only engines powerful enough to blast a payload into
orbit and work beyond the atmosphere. The United
States and the Soviet Union competed in a space race
to put a person on the moon. On July 20, 1969, the
U.S. *Apollo 11* mission landed the
first astronauts there. Today's
space vehicles, such as the
space shuttle, are still
propelled by rockets.

Shuttle mission
The space shuttle takes off like a rocket but
lands like a glider on a runway. The first space
shuttle, *Columbia*, was launched in 1981.

Rocket plane

Neil Armstrong, who later became the first person to set foot on the moon, stands in front of the experimental rocket-plane X-15. Between 1959 and 1968 it made scores of flights to the edge of the atmosphere.

Resisting heat

The space shuttle orbiter reenters the atmosphere at 16,000 mph (26,000km/h)—or 25 times the speed of sound. Friction between the orbiter and the air rushing past create very high temperatures. The space shuttle is covered with 20,000 heat-resistant glass tiles. The hottest parts of the shuttle—the nose and the front edges of the wing—are made from carbon and designed to withstand temperatures of 2,300°F (1,260°C).

Blastoff

At blastoff the space shuttle's three main engines and two booster rockets provide thrust equivalent to 140 jumbo jets.

Flying into the future

Aircraft have developed at an astonishing pace since the Wright brothers made the first airplane flight in 1903. The first supersonic flight, for example, followed only 44 years later. In the near future aircraft are set to become faster and even larger. The first "superjumbo" airliner, the Airbus A380, has now entered commercial service. And in 30 years' time there may be rocket-planes carrying passengers at more than ten times the speed of sound and flying so high that they skim the top of the atmosphere.

Experimental spaceplane
If spaceflight is to become commonplace, new spaceplanes will have to be less expensive to launch. The X-33 was designed as a half-size prototype for one of these craft. The project was canceled by NASA in 2001, but future spaceplanes will benefit from the research that went into it.

Hypersoar
By 2035 Hypersoar may be transporting passengers and cargo at speeds of up to 6,200 mph (10,000km/h). Hypersoar is designed to skip across the top of the atmosphere. As Hypersoar sinks back into the atmosphere a burst of engine power boosts it to the right height again. This unique trajectory will protect Hypersoar from excessive overheating in the atmosphere.

Faster airliners

Airline passengers want to get to their destinations as fast as possible, so a research group in the United States developed a concept for a new supersonic airliner for the 21st century. The proposed High Speed Civil Transport (HSCT) would halve flight times between the United States and the Far East or Europe. It would carry up to 300 passengers at Mach 2.4 (2.4 times the speed of sound). A flight in the HSCT from Los Angeles to Tokyo, Japan, would be six hours shorter than a normal subsonic flight. An HSCT flight in stages from Los Angeles to Sydney, Australia, would save ten hours on a subsonic flight today. The research project has been phased out, but it has taken the first steps toward the possibility of developing such an aircraft.

Superjumbo

The European aircraft manufacturer Airbus Industrie has developed the world's biggest airliner. The Airbus A380 is a giant airliner that can carry 555 passengers in three classes or up to 840 people in an all-economy-class layout. The A380 has been assembled in France. Its parts have been built in France, the U.K., Germany, and Spain.

Future airport

Tilt-rotor aircraft for short-haul flights could be a common sight at airports by 2010. Airports will need to evolve to meet the needs of new kinds of aircraft, as well as coping with the rise in air passenger numbers. Automated passenger handling systems such as passport control and security will reduce waiting time on the ground and prevent overcrowding.

X-33

Controlling an aircraft

Airplanes are able to fly because of the shape of their wings. Air flows faster over the curved top than across the flat underside. This creates a force called lift, which pulls the aircraft up. An airplane is steered by moving panels called control surfaces. There are three types—ailerons in the wings, and elevators and a rudder in the tail.

Steering
A plane is steered in three ways—pitch, roll, and yaw. Changing its pitch brings the nose up or down. Rolling it brings one wing up and the other down. Yaw turns the nose to the left or right.

Yaw right
Turning the rudder to the right by using the foot pedals pushes the tail fin in the opposite direction and swings the plane's nose around to the right.

Yaw left
Turning the rudder to the left pushes the tail fin in the opposite direction, swinging the plane's nose around to the left.

control column

propeller

rudder pedal

Pitch up
Pulling the control column back raises both elevators in the tail. Air pushing against them presses the tail down and brings the nose up.

Pitch down
Pushing the control column forward swings the elevators down. The airplane's tail rises and its nose tips down.

Turning

An airplane turns by raising one wing and lowering the other. A sideways pull swings the plane into a turn. The elevators and rudder are used to make small adjustments to keep the airplane level and pointing in the right direction during the turn.

rudder

tail fin

elevator

aileron

Jet engine
A turbofan jet engine has a propeller-like fan to suck air into the center of the engine. Here fuel is burned. Hot exhaust gases shoot out of the rear of the engine, pushing the plane forward.

lift

thrust

drag

weight

Fundamental forces
The same four forces act on all powered aircraft—lift, weight, thrust, and drag. When the lift created by the wings is greater than the weight of the aircraft, it takes off.

Streamlining
Aircraft are long, narrow, and smooth so that they can cut easily through the air. Shaping things like this is called streamlining.

Roll left
Turning the controls to the left, like a car steering wheel, moves the ailerons so that the right wing rises and the left wing sinks.

Roll right
Turning the controls to the right makes the right wing sink and left wing rise, pulling the plane around into a right turn.

Plane facts

From the smallest ultralight to the largest airliner, every type of aircraft has a unique set of personal statistics. These include its wingspan, length, and speed. On these pages you will find a selection of aircraft types, all pictured to scale. The huge variation in size, shape, and performance reflects the wide range of roles for which different aircraft are designed.

The Concorde
(no longer in service)
Speed: 1,335 mph (2,333km/h)
Passengers: up to 144
Crew: 3 (plus cabin crew)
Length: 204 ft. (62.1m)
Wingspan: 84 ft. (25.6m)

Learjet
Speed: 524 mph
(858km/h)
Passengers: 9
Crew: 2
Length: 55 ft. (17.9m)
Wingspan: 43 ft. (13.4m)

Northrop B-2 bomber
Speed: 474 mph (764km/h)
Passengers: 0
Crew: 2
Length: 69 ft. (21m)
Wingspan: 172 ft. (52.4m)

Boeing 747-400
Speed: 564 mph (910km/h)
Passengers: up to 568
Crew: 2 (plus cabin crew)
Length: 232 ft. (70.6m)
Wingspan: 211 ft. (64.4m)

Lockheed Martin F-22
Speed: more than 1,200 mph
(2,000km/h)
Passengers: 0
Crew: 1
Length: 62 ft. (18.9m)
Wingspan: 45 ft. (13.6m)

Airbus A300
Speed: 567 mph (891km/h)
Passengers: up to 375
Crew: 2 (plus cabin crew)
Length: 175 ft. (54.1m)
Wingspan: 147 ft. (44.8m)

Boeing Vertol Chinook
Speed: 160 mph (256km/h)
Passengers: up to 55
Crew: 2
Length: 51 ft. (15.5m) plus
rotors
Rotor diameter: 60 ft. (18.3m)

Bell/Boeing V-22 Osprey
Speed: 316 mph (509km/h)
Passengers: up to 24
Crew: 2
Length: 57 ft. (17.5m)
Wingspan: 51 ft. (15.5m)

Flying firsts

Most modern aircraft can trace their ancestry back to the Wright *Flyer*. New aircraft generally improve on existing models in small ways. They might be a little bit bigger or fly a little faster or higher. But from time to time innovations or breakthroughs are made that transform aircraft technology. For example, when Frank Whittle invented the jet engine in the 1940s, it revolutionized air transportation. And when Wernher von Braun and Sergei Korolev developed the world's biggest rockets after World War II, they made crewed spaceflight possible.

Leonardo da Vinci's drawings of flying machines
(1480s–1500)

Montgolfier hot-air balloon
First crewed flight
(1783)

Wright *Flyer*
First powered flight (1903)

Sikorsky VS-300
First modern helicopter
(1939)

George Cayley's glider
First heavier-than-air craft to carry a person (1849)

Messerschmitt Me 262
First jet fighter
(1942)

Henri Giffard's airship
First airship (1852)

Sputnik 1
First artificial satellite
(1957)

Apollo spacecraft
First crewed landing
on the moon (1969)

Space shuttle *Columbia*
First reusable crewed
spacecraft (1981)

Boeing 747
First and biggest wide-
bodied jet airliner (1969)

Breitling *Orbiter 3*
First nonstop around-
the-world balloon
flight (1999)

Bell X-1
First supersonic flight (1947)

Bell/Boeing V-22 Osprey
First tilt-rotor aircraft (1989)

Voyager
First nonstop
around-the-world
flight without
refueling (1986)

X-33 space plane
Experimental design for first single-
stage-to-orbit reusable aircraft

De Havilland DH106 Comet
First jet airliner (1949)

Airbus A380
World's biggest airliner (2005)

Glossary

ailerons Control surfaces in a plane's wings that tilt to make the plane roll to one side or the other.

air traffic control An organization that guides aircraft through the sky by monitoring their position using radar and giving pilots instructions by radio.

airframe The basic structure of an aircraft, not including its engines.

airplane A powered, heavier-than-air craft.

airship A powered, lighter-than-air craft.

altitude The height of an aircraft above sea level.

atmosphere The air that surrounds the earth.

biplane A plane with two sets of wings, one above the other.

black boxes Another name for the flight data recorder and the cockpit voice recorder. These two recorders are carried in airliners to provide clues to the cause of an accident.

blind flying Flying by using instruments only, because the view outside an aircraft has disappeared because of fog, cloud, or darkness.

civil aviation Nonmilitary flying.

cockpit The part of an aircraft where the pilot sits.

cockpit voice recorder (CVR) One of two recorders carried in an airliner. The CVR records everything the pilots say and can give vital clues if an accident happens.

combustion chamber The part of an engine where the fuel is burned.

control surfaces Movable panels on an aircraft that are used by the pilot to make the aircraft climb, turn, and dive.

dirigible Another name for an airship.

dogfight Close combat between fighter planes as they chase each other and try to shoot each other down.

drag Another name for air resistance, or the tendency of air to slow down anything that tries to fly through it.

ejector seat A seat in a fighter plane that blasts the pilot to safety in an emergency. Once clear of the aircraft the pilot lands by parachute.

elevators Control surfaces in a plane's tail that tilt to make the tail rise or fall. This makes the plane dive or climb.

elevon A control surface used by delta-wing planes that works as both an elevator and aileron.

fixed-wing aircraft Aircraft with wings that do not move, unlike helicopters, which have spinning rotors.

flaps Panels that slide out from the airplane's wings to make them bigger. This helps provide more lift when the plane is flying slowly after takeoff and before landing.

flight data recorder One of the two recorders carried by an airliner to give clues to the cause of an accident. The other recorder is the cockpit voice recorder.

flight deck The part of a large aircraft, such as an airliner, where the crew sits.

flight envelope The range of speeds and heights within which an aircraft can fly safely.

flight simulator A copy of an aircraft's cockpit or flight deck used to train and test pilots. The simulator moves, and the pilots see computer-generated views to make "flying" the simulator as realistic as possible.

flying boat A plane with a watertight, boat-shaped hull designed to land in water.

flying wing A plane shaped like a large wing.

fuselage Another name for the main body of a plane.

G suit A tight suit worn by a fighter pilot. The suit inflates like a balloon to squeeze the pilot's lower body and legs to stop blood draining away from the head during tight turns.

gas turbine Another name for the jet engine, a turbine engine driven by gas. The gas is produced by burning fuel inside the engine.

glider An unpowered, fixed-wing aircraft.

global positioning system (GPS) A navigation system that enables pilots and others to locate their position very accurately by using radio signals from satellites.

hangar A building where aircraft are housed and stored.

hang glider An unpowered aircraft made from a wing, from which the pilot hangs and steers by moving their body.

helipad An open space set aside for helicopters to land and to take off.

landing gear An aircraft's wheels, or undercarriage.

lift An upward-acting force produced by an aircraft that enables it to take off and fly. Lift can be produced by wings, rotor blades, engine thrust, or a lighter-than-air gas.

lighter-than-air craft Aircraft that produce lift by carrying a large bag of gas, such as hot air, hydrogen, or helium, that is lighter than the surrounding air.

microburst A strong wind blowing down from the base of a thunderstorm. A microburst can cause a sudden change in wind direction called wind shear.

monoplane A fixed-wing aircraft with one wing across the top or on each side.

navigation Steering a course to find the way from one place to another.

piston engine A type of engine used by the smallest planes and helicopters that works like a car engine. Fuel burned inside cylinders forces pistons down the cylinders to turn a propeller or rotor.

pitch A movement of an aircraft that tilts its nose up or down.

pylon 1) A post attached to an aircraft's wing for attaching an engine or weapons. 2) A tower used to mark out a course for air races.

radar A system for locating aircraft by sending out bursts of radio signals and detecting any reflections that bounce back.

retractable wheels Wheels that fold up inside an aircraft when it takes off.

rocket A vehicle propelled by one or more rocket motors.

rocket motor An engine that produces thrust, such as a jet engine. The rocket engine carries its own supply of oxygen to enable it to burn its fuel without any need to take in air.

roll The banking movement of an aircraft in which one wing rises and the other falls.

rotor A set of rotating, wing-shaped blades. A spinning rotor provides lift for a helicopter.

rotorcraft An aircraft powered by one or more rotors, such as a helicopter.

rudder A control surface in an aircraft's tail fin that swivels to the left or right to turn the plane in a particular direction.

satellite An object that circles a planet. The moon is a natural satellite of the earth. A spacecraft orbiting the earth is an artificial satellite.

seaplane A plane fitted with floats so that it can land on water. It is sometimes called a float plane.

speed of sound The speed at which sound travels. It varies according to air temperature. At sea level it is about 698 mph (1,125km/h). At higher altitudes, where it is colder, the speed of sound drops to about 658 mph (1,060km/h).

stealth plane A military plane that is designed to be difficult to detect by radar.

subsonic Slower than the speed of sound.

supersonic Faster than the speed of sound.

tailplane The small, winglike panels in the tail of an aircraft.

thermal A rising current of warm air. Thermals are used by glider pilots to climb higher. A glider circling inside a thermal is carried up with the rising air.

thrust The force produced by an aircraft's engine or a rocket motor to make an aircraft or spacecraft move.

turbofan An efficient type of jet engine that has a large, spinning fan at the front to suck air into the engine.

turboprop A type of jet engine that drives a propeller.

ultralight A small, lightweight recreational aircraft, often with an open cockpit, capable of carrying one or two people.

wind shear A sudden change in wind direction.

yaw A turn to the left or right.

Index

Acknowledgments

The publishers would like to thank the following
illustrators for their contributions to this book:
b = bottom, c = center, l = left, r = right, t = top, m = middle

Julian Baker 8 *m, 21 tr, 26–27, 29 tr 50 tr;* **Julian Baum** 52 *bl;* **Mark Bergin** 1 *c,* 12–13, 14–15, 16–17,
18–19, 20–21, 24–25, 36–37, 44–45; **Nick Clifford** 53 *mr;* **Tom Connell** cover, 4–5, 28–29, 32–33, 50–51;
Sidney Coulridge 30–31; **Mike Davis** 32 *bl;* **Alan Hancocks** 10–11, 22–23, 40–41, 46–47, 54–55, 56–57;
John James 38–39, 42–43; **B Knight** 33 *mr;* **Chris Lion** 22 *tl;* **Kevin Maddison** 6–7, 8–9, 27*tl,* 34–35, 48–49,
58–59; **David Russell** 55 *tr.*

The publishers would also like to thank the following for supplying photographs for this book:
6 *tr* TRH; **7** *t* Quadrant Picture Library; **8** *tl* Quadrant Picture Library, *br* Science Photo Library/Philippe
Gontier/Eurelios/Onera; **11** *tc* Quadrant Picture Library/Simon Everett; **12** *t* Corbis; *c* TRH; **14** *cl* Corbis; **15** *tc* Corbis;
c TRH/Canadair; **16** *t* Hulton Getty; **18** *cl* TRH/R Winslade; **19** *t* Science & Society Picture Library/George
Woodbine/Daily Herald Archive/NMPFT, *tr* TRH; **20** *tl* Corbis; **21** *tl* Corbis, *br* The Aviation Picture Library; **22** *br*
Popperfoto; **25** *tr* NASA; **26** *br* Corbis; **28** *tl* Royal Aeronautical Society, *cl* The Aviation Picture Library; **29** *c* Quadrant
Picture Library *b,* Topham Picture Point; **30** *tl* Royal Aeronautical Society, *bc* Royal Aeronautical Society; **35** *tr*
Quadrant Picture Library *cr,* TRH/British Aerospace; **36** *tr* Quadrant Picture Library/Erik Simonsen, 1994, *bl* The
Aviation Picture Library/Northrop Grumman; **37** *tr* The Aviation Picture Library; **38** *tl* Science & Society Picture
Library/Science Museum, *bl* The Aviation Picture Library/Patrick Darphin; **39** *tr* NASA; **42** *tl* TRH//Munich Museum;
43 *tl* Science Photo Library/United States Library of Congress, *cr* Hulton Getty; **44** *bl* (center) Science & Society
Picture Library/Daily Herald Archive/NMPFT, *bl* Corbis/Underwood & Underwood *bc* Corbis *br* Science & Society
Picture Library/DHA/NMPFT; **45** *tc* The Aviation Picture Library; **46** *cl* NASA; **47** *b* NASA; **48** *br* Royal Aeronautical
Society; **49** *r* The Aviation Picture Library, *bl* The Aviation Picture Library, *bc* Rex Features; **50** *tc* Science Photo
Library/NASA; **51** *tl* NASA; **52–53** *c* NASA; **53** *tr* Rex Features.

Every effort has been made to trace the copyright holders of the photographs.
The publishers apologize for any inconvenience caused.

Below is a list of useful web sites:

www.nasm.edu (Smithsonian National Air & Space Museum, Washington, D.C.)
www.naval-air.org (National Museum of Naval Aviation at the Naval Air Station, Pensacola, FL)
www.iwasm.org (International Women's Air & Space Museum, Cleveland, OH)
www.nasa.gov (NASA aviation and space site)
www.dfrc.nasa.gov (NASA's Dryden Flight Research Center home page)
www.sprucegoose.org (Hughes HK-1 "Spruce Goose" site)
www.eaa.org (Experimental Aircraft Association for homebuilt and
experimental aircraft constructors and pilots)
www.airmuseum.org (International Sport Aviation Museum, Lakeland, FL)
www.aloha.net/~icarus (Aloha Flight 243 accident)
spaceflight.nasa.gov (Space shuttle/space station)